BATTLES

OF THE REVOLUTIONARY WAR

PATRICK CATEL

Heinemann Library
Chicago, Illinois

www.heinemannraintree.com
Visit our website to find out
more information about
Heinemann-Raintree books.

To order:
☎ Phone 888-454-2279
🖥 Visit www.heinemannraintree.com
to browse our catalog and order online.

©2011 Heinemann Library
an imprint of Capstone Global Library, LLC
Chicago, Illinois

Edited by Megan Cotugno
Designed by Ryan Frieson
Picture research by Tracy Cummins
Originated by Capstone Global Library
Printed and bound in the United States of America,
North Mankato, MN.

14 13 12
10 9 8 7 6 5 4 3

Library of Congress Cataloging-in-Publication Data

Catel, Patrick.
  Battles of the Revolutionary War / Patrick Catel.
    p. cm. — (Why we fought : the Revolutionary War)
  Includes bibliographical references and index.
  ISBN 978-1-4329-3896-3 (hardcover)
  ISBN 978-1-4329-3901-4 (paperback)

  1. United States—History—Revolution,
1775-1783—Campaigns—Juvenile literature. I. Title.
  E230.C38 2011
  973.3'3—dc22
  102012   2009050071
  006969

Acknowledgments

The author and publishers are grateful to the following for
permission to reproduce copyright material:

Library of Congress Prints and Photographs Division pp. 5,
12, 15, 30, 32, 34, 35, 41, 43; North Wind Picture Archives
p. 10 (© North Wind); Shutterstock p. 22; The Art Archive
pp. 20 (Gift of Mrs. Arthur H. Scribner in memory of her
husband / Museum of the City of New York / 41.62.106), 33;
The Bridgeman Art Library International pp. 6 (Delaware Art
Museum, Wilmington, USA / Howard Pyle Collection), 16
(© Collection of the New-York Historical Society, USA), 26
(Peter Newark American Pictures), 40 (Gudin, Jean Antoine
Theodore); The Granger Collection, New York pp. 9, 18, 21,
24, 25, 29, 36, 37, 39.

Cover photo of Battle Of Concord Bridge, 1775 reproduced
with permission of SuperStock (© SuperStock).

We would like to thank Dr. Edward Cook for his invaluable
help in the preparation of this book.

Contents

Throughout this book, you will find green text boxes that contain facts and questions to help you interact with a primary source. Use these questions as a way to think more about where our historical information comes from.

Some words are shown in bold, **like this**. You can find out what they mean by looking in the glossary, on page 46.

Why Did We Fight the Revolutionary War?

Today, the United States of America is known as one of the strongest nations in the world. This can make it difficult to imagine how close the **colonies** came to failing in their revolution. The supporters of the Declaration of Independence risked their lives in a **rebellion** against Great Britain in 1776.

In 1760, George III became king of Great Britain. He signed the Treaty of Paris with France in 1763 to end the **French and Indian War**. The British gained control of Canada and the land east of the Mississippi River. However, Great Britain had a large debt from the war.

British Taxes and Colonial Anger

King George III and the British **Parliament** felt colonists in North America should help pay for the French and Indian War and the protection provided by British troops. Great Britain began to pass acts (laws) that required the colonists to pay taxes. These included the **Sugar Act** in 1764, the **Stamp Act** in 1765, the **Townshend Acts** in 1767, the **Tea Act** in 1773, and the **Intolerable Acts** in 1774. The colonies responded by protesting and **boycotting** British goods. Colonists also formed committees and groups such as the **Sons of Liberty** to take action against the acts.

Events turned violent in Boston in 1770, when British troops fired on a rowdy crowd that was protesting British policies. Samuel Adams called it the "Boston Massacre." He used the event to gain support for the cause of American independence. The more the colonists protested British taxes, the more King George III refused to budge. The king ordered General Thomas Gage to use military force to keep control in Massachusetts. In 1775, months before the signing of the Declaration of Independence, the Revolutionary War had already begun.

THE BATTLE of BUNKER'S HILL.

Primary Source: The Battle of Bunker Hill

The **Patriots** faced one of the largest and most disciplined military forces in the world. At the Battle of Bunker Hill in June 1775, the Patriots held their own against the mighty British forces.

Thinking About the Source:

What is happening in this image?

What can you learn from examining this image?

If this picture were created today, what would be different?

What Happened at Lexington and Concord?

Patrick Henry's famous phrase, "Give me liberty or give me death," expressed how many colonists felt in the spring of 1775. British General Thomas Gage was under pressure from British leaders to act with force to keep Britain's control in the **colonies**. The **Patriots** had many spies in Boston. Rumors spread around Massachusetts that the British would soon march on Concord. Colonists began moving weapons and supplies out of the town.

KEYS TO VICTORY

In April 1775, the **Continental Congress** had not yet approved the formation of a national army. Instead, each colony had its own **militia**, which was made up of citizen soldiers. Most were volunteers who normally worked in other trades and jobs. Minutemen volunteered or were picked from the militias. They were called "minutemen" because they were expected to be ready to march or fight with only a minute's notice.

The British Are Coming!

On the evening of April 18, 1775, a group of 800 British troops headed north toward Concord. Their plan was to quickly grab weapons stored there. They also hoped to arrest Samuel Adams and John Hancock along the way. British spies knew that Adams and Hancock could be found in Lexington. Paul Revere and William Dawes learned of this plan. They left Boston on horseback to warn colonists that the British were coming.

It is not known for certain which side fired the first shot at Lexington. That shot became known as "the shot heard 'round the world."

The Patriots Are Warned

Revere and Dawes arrived in Lexington first with their warning. Adams and Hancock were able to escape, and the militiamen were called to fight. The British troops marched 24 kilometers (15 miles) from Boston to Lexington. When they arrived, about 70 militiamen stood ready to defend the town. At the head of the British troops, Major John Pitcairn ordered the militiamen to throw down their weapons.

This map shows some of the major battle sites of the Revolutionary War. Lexington and Concord are in the upper right hand corner of the map.

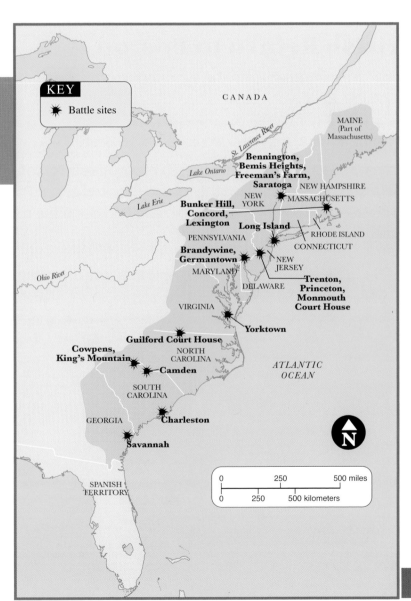

KEY

★ Battle sites

CANADA

MAINE
(Part of Massachusetts)

St. Lawrence River

Lake Ontario

Bennington,
Bemis Heights,
Freeman's Farm,
Saratoga

NEW HAMPSHIRE

NEW
YORK

MASSACHUSETTS

Lake Erie

Bunker Hill,
Concord,
Lexington

Long Island

RHODE ISLAND

PENNSYLVANIA

CONNECTICUT

Brandywine,
Germantown

NEW
JERSEY

Ohio River

MARYLAND

DELAWARE

Trenton,
Princeton,
Monmouth
Court House

VIRGINIA

Yorktown

Guilford Court House

Cowpens,
King's Mountain

NORTH
CAROLINA

ATLANTIC
OCEAN

Camden

SOUTH
CAROLINA

GEORGIA

Charleston

Savannah

N

SPANISH
TERRITORY

0		250		500 miles

0	250	500 kilometers

Shot Heard 'Round the World

On the colonists' side, Captain John Parker commanded 70 **militiamen** against 800 British troops. Seeing that they were greatly outnumbered, Parker ordered his men to disperse (move apart). Some refused, but many followed his orders. As they walked away, a shot rang out. A series of shots then followed from the British.

Eight militiamen were killed and nine were wounded. Order was restored, and the British continued their march west to Concord. When the British troops arrived in Concord, they searched the town. However, almost all weapons and ammunition had already been removed by the colonists.

British Return to Boston

Meanwhile, militiamen from the surrounding area arrived. They met at the north bridge leading into Concord. A small group of British soldiers was guarding the bridge. The militiamen outnumbered them and decided to attack. The British retreated back into town. From there, they decided to return to Boston.

On the way back to Boston, the British received **reinforcements**. The British made easy targets, marching down the road in their red coats. The **colonial** militiamen hid behind trees and anything else they could find along the route the British took, firing on them as they retreated to Boston.

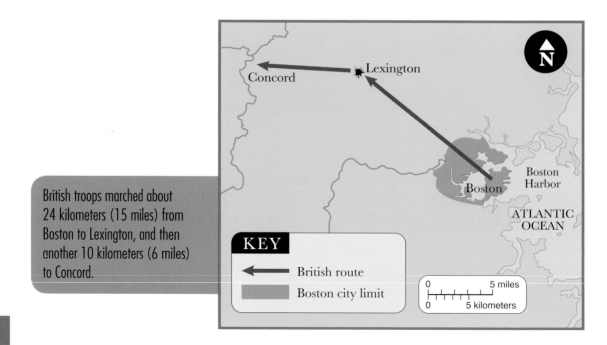

British troops marched about 24 kilometers (15 miles) from Boston to Lexington, and then another 10 kilometers (6 miles) to Concord.

KEY

← British route

Boston city limit

By the time they reached Charlestown, north of Boston, the British had 73 killed, 174 wounded, and 26 missing. **Patriot** losses were 49 dead, 39 wounded, and 4 missing. Volunteer militiamen had kept over 1,500 professional British soldiers on the run. The battles of the Revolutionary War had begun.

KEYS TO VICTORY

The colonial militias had a lot of support from the population in **New England**. Spies there made sure militiamen knew when the British were on the move. That's why militiamen were able to attack the British while they retreated to Boston after Lexington and Concord.

Militiamen used **guerilla** attacks on the British as they retreated to Boston.

Why Was Fort Ticonderoga Important?

Once the British retreated to Boston, more **militiamen** gathered around the city. The **Patriots** soon realized they did not have the cannons and ammunition they would need to complete a **siege** of Boston. Benedict Arnold offered to lead an expedition (mission) to Lake Champlain against British forts there. If he could capture Fort Ticonderoga, the Patriots would have its cannons and ammunition.

Arnold was made a colonel. He recruited a few hundred men and headed out for Lake Champlain. Arnold learned that Ethan Allen was also planning to take Fort Ticonderoga. Allen was the leader of a militia group called the Green Mountain Boys. Arnold joined forces with Allen 3.2 kilometers (2 miles) below Fort Ticonderoga. They rowed across the lake with about 80 men for a surprise attack at daybreak on May 10, 1775.

Ethan Allen, Benedict Arnold, and the Green Mountain Boys easily captured Fort Ticonderoga in a surprise attack. Only one Patriot was injured.

British Surrender

The British commander, Captain William De la Place, was extremely surprised. He surrendered the fort. The Patriots now had almost 100 cannons and other various supplies. The American people celebrated the good news of the first American victory at Fort Ticonderoga. Ethan Allen quickly became a hero. Benedict Arnold was angry that he received very little credit, or attention, for his actions.

The victory at Fort Ticonderoga was important for the Patriots. The cannons and supplies that were captured were later used in the siege of Boston. The capture of Fort Ticonderoga also helped protect the **colonies** against a British invasion that might come from Canada.

WHAT WENT WRONG?

Later in the Revolutionary War, Benedict Arnold became a **traitor**. He tried to hand West Point, an important fort, over to the British. The plan failed, but Arnold escaped and fought for the British during the rest of the war.

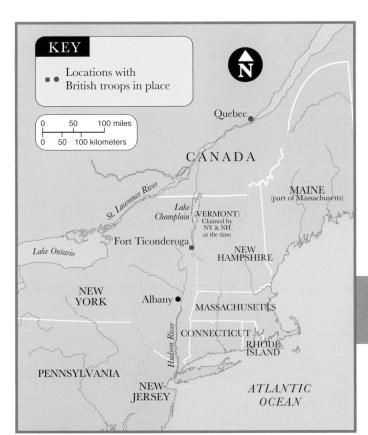

KEY

■ ● Locations with British troops in place

0   50   100 miles
0   50   100 kilometers

Quebec

CANADA

St. Lawrence River

Lake Champlain

MAINE
(part of Massachusetts)

(VERMONT)
Claimed by NY & NH at the time

Fort Ticonderoga

Lake Ontario

NEW HAMPSHIRE

NEW YORK

Albany

MASSACHUSETTS

Hudson River

CONNECTICUT

RHODE ISLAND

PENNSYLVANIA

NEW JERSEY

ATLANTIC OCEAN

Fort Ticonderoga was located in a strategic (important) position on Lake Champlain.

What Happened at the Battle of Bunker Hill?

Through the night of June 16 and into the early morning of June 17 in 1775, **colonial militiamen** positioned themselves on Breed's Hill, across the bay from Boston. They worked through the night to create better defenses for their positions. The British in Boston saw the colonial defenses the morning of June 17 and planned an attack.

The British lost many soldiers while climbing Breed's Hill during the fight against the Americans.

British General Gage ordered William Howe to send soldiers across the river to attack the militiamen on Breed's Hill. The British boats landed, and lines of foot soldiers attacked. Warships and **artillery** supported them. The British had to climb a hill to attack the colonists, who stood their ground and were well protected. The British loss of soldiers was large.

Victory?

Reinforcements arrived for the British. They attacked a third time. The Americans were out of ammunition. They were forced to retreat to Bunker Hill, and then northwest back to the mainland. The British had taken the hill, but nearly half of their troops were killed or wounded. The Battle of Bunker Hill is seen as a colonial victory for that reason.

Siege of Boston

In June 1775, the second **Continental Congress** agreed to form a Continental Army. They appointed George Washington as the commander in chief. Washington met his army and saw that the men needed training and discipline. More importantly, they were in need of ammunition. Henry Knox saved the day when he showed up that winter with cannons and supplies taken from Fort Ticonderoga.

Over three nights in March 1776, Continental soldiers occupied high ground overlooking Boston and built defenses. With American cannons in place on the hills, the British decided to leave Boston.

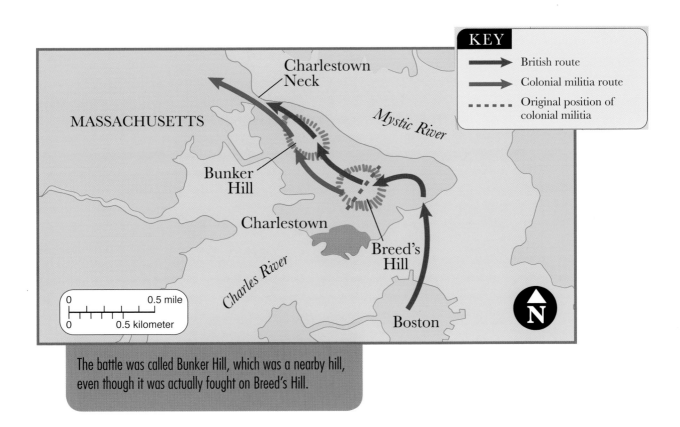

The battle was called Bunker Hill, which was a nearby hill, even though it was actually fought on Breed's Hill.

What Fighting Happened in Quebec, Canada?

While Washington waited outside Boston in the winter of 1775–1776, a group of about 1,000 volunteer **Patriot** troops under the command of Benedict Arnold marched toward Canada. Their goal was to take the Canadian **territory** from the British. They marched through thick forests during harsh winter weather. Hundreds of men died along the way from disease and starvation.

Battle of Quebec

Another Patriot force led by General Richard Montgomery invaded Canada from New York. They took Montreal from the British, and then met up with Arnold and his men outside of Quebec City. The British inside Quebec refused to surrender. After a long **siege**, the Americans made a surprise attack in the very early morning of December 31, 1775.

WHAT WENT WRONG FOR THE PATRIOTS?

After Benedict Arnold was wounded at the Battle of Quebec, Daniel Morgan took command. His second attack broke through into the lower part of Quebec City. However, at that point his men paused, instead of pursuing, or following, the British. They decided to wait for General Montgomery. They did not know that Montgomery had already been killed in the fighting. As the Patriots waited, the British were able to regroup and make a counterattack. Morgan and his men were forced to either surrender or retreat across the frozen St. Lawrence River. Many soldiers surrendered.

The British had recently received **reinforcements** and put up a fierce defense. General Montgomery was killed in the fighting. Benedict Arnold was wounded during a charge. Over 400 Patriots were captured, and about 60 were wounded or killed. The wounded Arnold and his remaining men were forced to withdraw. Victory went to the British, who kept control of Quebec.

In May 1776, the Patriot troops began to withdraw from Canada. By the end of June 1776, all Patriot troops were out of Canada. No fighting between **colonial** and British forces took place in Canada for the rest of the Revolutionary War.

COLONEL ARNOLD.
Who Commanded the Provincial Troops sent against QUEBEC, through the Wilderness of Canada, and was Wounded in Storming that City, under General Montgomery.
London, Published as the Act directs 26 March 1776 by Tho. Hart.

Primary Source: Benedict Arnold

Benedict Arnold was a hero for the Patriots early in the Revolutionary War. He would go on to become the most famous **traitor** in American history.

Thinking About the Source:

What words can you see in this image?

Do you think this portrait of Arnold was made before or after Arnold became a traitor to the Patriots?

What Was Happening at Sea?

In October 1775, the **Continental Congress** created the Continental Navy. On March 1, 1776, **Commodore** Esek Hopkins took all eight ships of the new Continental Navy to the Bahamas. Hopkins then sailed toward the forts protecting the Port of Nassau. Hopkins' men attacked and captured both forts. They loaded weapons and ammunition onto the Continental ships and set sail for the **colonies**.

Hopkins's fleet arrived off the coast of Rhode Island on April 4, 1776. They met and captured two British warships, the *Hawk* and the *Bolton*. Hopkins learned that the British fleet was sailing nearby. He and Captain John Hazard fought and pursued the *Glasgow*, a single British warship, but the ship was able to escape. Hopkins and Hazard were removed from their positions for their poor performance. John Paul Jones took over command of Hazard's ship, the *Providence*.

Congress bought **merchant** ships and mounted cannons on them, in order to use them as warships. They were no match for the British warships.

Battle of Lake Champlain

While fighting the British in Canada, Benedict Arnold discovered that they planned to invade New York and attack George Washington's army. Their plan was to sail across Lake Champlain and then down to New York in ships built to travel in shallow water.

Arnold knew he could not defeat the British. However, if he could hold off the British advance until winter weather arrived, they would have to give up the invasion until the following spring.

Arnold and his men built 15 small, fast ships by September 1776. Arnold and his ships were able to damage the British ships on Lake Champlain on October 11, 1776, before escaping. The British had to take time to repair the damage. Winter weather arrived, and Arnold was successful in delaying the British invasion of New York. This gave Washington time to strengthen and train his army.

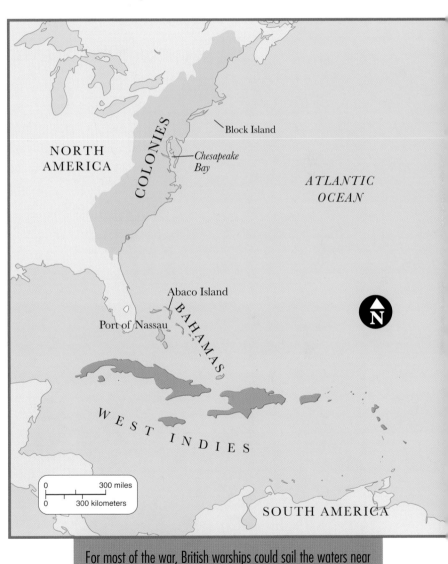

For most of the war, British warships could sail the waters near the **colonies** without fear of the Continental Navy.

How Did New York Fall to the British?

The British decided to make New York City their headquarters, as George Washington suspected they would. In August 1776, Washington positioned much of his army on Long Island to protect New York City from attack. British General William Howe noticed a weak point in the colonial line and sent a force to attack.

KEYS TO VICTORY

The British increased the size of their army by hiring troops from other parts of Europe. This was a common practice at the time. Almost 17,000 soldiers from the German state of Hesse-Cassel came to help the British fight. Great Britain paid Prince Frederick II for the use of his **Hessian** soldiers. About 8,000 Hessians fought for the British in New York in 1776. The experienced Hessians were a key to the British victory in New York City.

During the fighting in New York, Washington realized he had to retreat in order to live to fight another day.

Battle of Long Island

In the Battle of Long Island, the British overpowered the colonial troops. After the battle, Howe decided not to pursue Washington's army. It was a lucky break, but Washington knew he had to get his army off of Long Island. The Continental troops left their campfires burning, to fool the British. They made their escape across the East River into Manhattan. They were lucky again when a fog came early in the morning to cover the last of their escape.

Washington positioned troops around New York City. They were clearly outnumbered by the British. When British and Hessian soldiers landed in lower Manhattan, the colonial troops fled. Washington tried to rally his men, but he was forced to organize a quick retreat. They fell back to Harlem Heights, where they fought another battle the next day. The Continental soldiers fought bravely this time. However, the British continued to receive **reinforcements**. The Continental Army again had to retreat. Washington headed north to White Plains, New York.

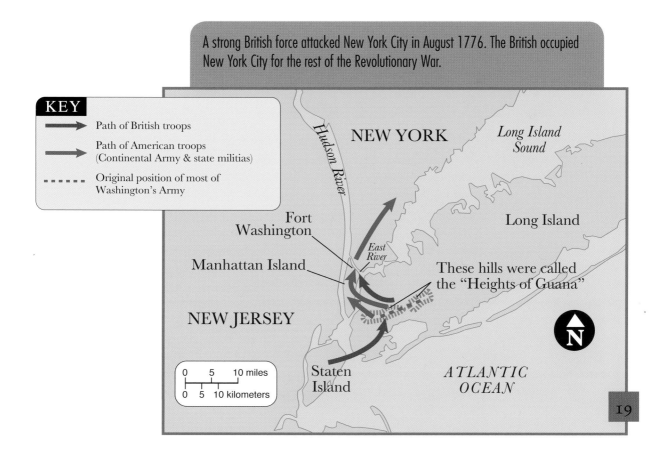

A strong British force attacked New York City in August 1776. The British occupied New York City for the rest of the Revolutionary War.

KEY

→ Path of British troops

→ Path of American troops (Continental Army & state militias)

----- Original position of most of Washington's Army

Hudson River

NEW YORK

Long Island Sound

Fort Washington

East River

Long Island

Manhattan Island

These hills were called the "Heights of Guana"

NEW JERSEY

N

0 5 10 miles
0 5 10 kilometers

Staten Island

ATLANTIC OCEAN

Battle of White Plains

On October 28, 1776, the Americans again met the British and **Hessian** soldiers in battle at White Plains, New York. The British eventually forced the Americans to fall back. British General Howe then stopped his advance, waiting for **reinforcements**. British reinforcements arrived, but a storm came and delayed their attack. When the storm stopped, Washington saw the British troops and realized he could not win. The Continental Army escaped overnight under the cover of darkness.

WHAT WENT WRONG?

The **militiamen** had to defend all of New York City. Since Manhattan is surrounded by water, the British could come by ship and land anywhere. When the attack came, the nervous **colonial** troops ran. It is said that George Washington rushed to the fighting on horseback when he heard the first shots. When he saw his troops fleeing in panic, Washington tried to stop them. He was furious and lashed out at them with his riding whip. Washington finally gave up and retreated, barely avoiding being overtaken by British forces.

The Continental Army had even fewer supplies because of the British capture of Fort Washington. Below is a view of the attack at Fort Washington.

View of the attack against Fort Washington and Rebel Redoubts near New York on the 16 of November 1776 by the British and Hessian Brigade. Drawn on the Spot by The Davies Esq. R.A. of Artillery.

Fall of Fort Washington

When Washington's army retreated from Manhattan, about 3,000 troops were left behind to defend Fort Washington. After sailing up the Hudson River, the British took Fort Washington on November 16, 1776. Most of the 3,000 colonial defenders were captured. The Americans also lost valuable weapons and supplies. By September 1776, British troops had taken over all of New York City. The British controlled New York City for the rest of the war.

Washington and his officers decided that he should take most of the army and retreat into New Jersey. British General Lord Charles Cornwallis pursued Washington's army through New Jersey. In December 1776, Washington and his army crossed the Delaware River into Pennsylvania. They used all the boats they could gather from the area, so the British were unable to follow.

New York City proved too difficult to defend, and Washington was forced to retreat.

How Did Washington Win at Trenton and Princeton?

Winter weather had now come. Many Continental soldiers wanted to go home. Some were planning to leave at the end of the year, when their period of **enlistment** ended. General Washington needed to find a way to encourage the soldiers to stay. He badly needed a victory.

On December 25, 1776, the Delaware River was filled with chunks of ice. There was a snow storm. That evening, George Washington and about 2,400 of his troops, with 18 cannons, rowed across the river into New Jersey. Once the troops landed, they marched nearly 14.4 kilometers (9 miles) across ice and snow to reach Trenton. The men and **artillery** split and approached the town from two roads.

WHAT WENT WRONG?

Washington wrote to the **Continental Congress** about his difficulties recruiting men, especially good officers. In a letter on September 24, 1776, to John Hancock, president of the Continental Congress, Washington wrote:

"As the war must be carried on systematically, and to do it, you must have good officers, there are, in my judgment, no other possible means to obtain them but by establishing your army upon a permanent footing, and giving your officers good pay."

John Fitzgerald described Washington as the last troops finished crossing the Delaware River: "I have never seen Washington so determined as he is now. He stands on the bank of the river, wrapped in his cloak, superintending [managing] the landing of his troops."

A Terrible Night

Colonel John Fitzgerald recorded the events that night, December 25, 1776:

"It is fearfully cold and raw, and a snowstorm setting in. The wind is northeast and beats in the faces of the men. It will be a terrible night for the soldiers who have no shoes. Some of them have tied old rags around their feet; others are barefoot, but I have not heard a man complain. They are ready to suffer any hardship and die rather than give up their liberty."

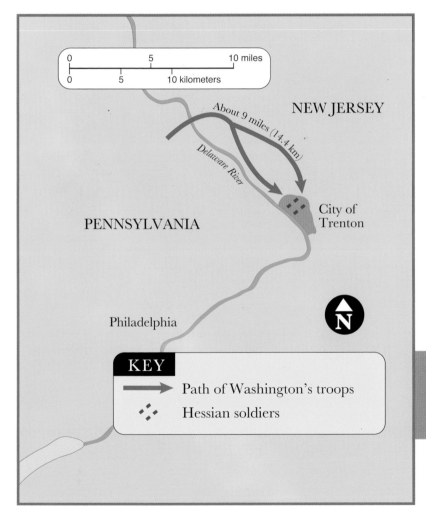

Colonial troops marched to Trenton after spending the night crossing the icy Delaware River.

Battle of Trenton

Early the next morning, Washington's men surprised the **Hessian** soldiers in Trenton. Many of the muskets and **artillery** were soaked from the freezing rain, so most soldiers used **bayonets** in the battle. The Hessians surrendered with little resistance.

The **Patriots** captured their valuable weapons and ammunition. More than 900 Hessian prisoners were taken back across the Delaware River and marched through Philadelphia. The **colonial** volunteers had defeated professional soldiers.

George Washington tried to convince Hessian soldiers to join the American side in the war.

KEYS TO VICTORY

A day after the colonial victory, on December 27, 1776, Colonel Fitzgerald wrote of its effect:

"It is a glorious victory. It will rejoice the hearts of our friends everywhere and give new life to our hitherto waning fortunes. Washington has baffled the enemy in his retreat from New York. He has pounced upon the Hessians like an eagle upon a hen and is safe once more on this side of the river."

Battle of Princeton

A week later, the Continental soldiers again crossed the Delaware River near Trenton. By
this time, Lord Cornwallis was on his way to meet them with British troops. His march
was slowed by the muddiness of the roads, caused by the recent ice storm. Continental
riflemen also slowed the British, using **guerilla** attacks like they did at the beginning of
the war. The colonial army went around the British using a side road they knew about.
They defeated the **garrison** at Princeton, and then retreated into the western part of
New Jersey to rest for the winter.

Victories at Trenton and Princeton encouraged Washington's troops and gave men a
reason to join the Continental Army. The British withdrew from most of New Jersey.
British General Howe stayed in his winter quarters in New York City through the spring.
However, he was then determined to take Philadelphia from the colonial troops.

What Happened During the Fighting in Pennsylvania?

In 1777, Philadelphia, Pennsylvania, was the largest city in North America, with more than 30,000 people. It was also the **colonial** capital and home of the **Continental Congress**. The British did not want the Continental Army to control this supply base. British General Sir William Howe left New York City in July 1777. He was determined to stop Washington and gain control of Philadelphia. Washington realized Howe's plan and moved his army to protect Philadelphia.

Battle of Brandywine

Howe sailed his troops toward Philadelphia. The British landed in Maryland and marched north. Washington led his troops south through Philadelphia. Howe sent **Hessian** soldiers to attack the center of Washington's battle line. Generals Howe and Cornwallis crossed Brandywine Creek and attacked the right side of Washington's line. As darkness fell, the tired Continental troops retreated. The victory at Brandywine went to the British on September 11, 1777.

The British were victorious in the Battle of Brandywine in September 1777. They marched into Philadelphia less than two weeks later.

British Capture Philadelphia

When they learned of Washington's defeat, the Continental Congress called for **reinforcements** from the surrounding colonies. It was too late for the city, however.

Over the next few weeks, a number of smaller battles took place. The British moved closer to Philadelphia. Members of the Continental Congress fled. Philadelphia was left undefended. The British marched into the city and took control on September 26, 1777.

Surprise Attack at Germantown

Most of the British Army was still camped 8 kilometers (5 miles) north of Philadelphia in a town called Germantown. Washington tried a surprise attack on October 4, 1777. The battle went well for the **Patriots** at first, but the British pulled together and gained strength. A thick fog caused confusion, and the colonial troops fell back. In November, the Continental Army gave up its defensive positions around Philadelphia.

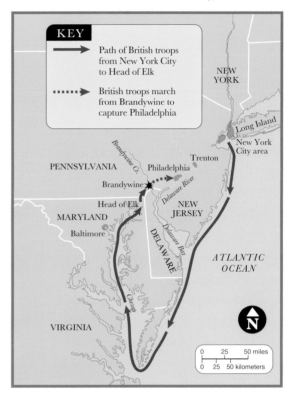

Top Map: General Howe sailed his British troops from New York City to the town of Head of Elk (now Elkton), Maryland. After landing, they marched north to Brandywine.

Bottom Map: Washington's army suffered about 1,000 casualties at Germantown. British casualties numbered about 500.

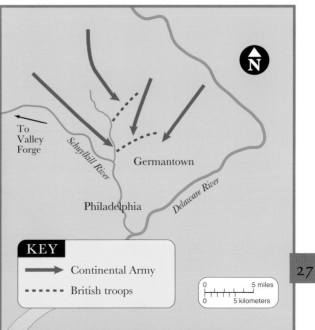

27

What Was the Turning Point in the War?

General Washington was most concerned with protecting Philadelphia from General Howe in the summer of 1777. However, he received news about another British force gathering in Quebec, Canada, led by General John Burgoyne. In addition to professional British soldiers, Burgoyne's force included **Hessian** soldiers, Canadian **Loyalists**, and Native Americans.

Battle of Bennington

Burgoyne led his troops out of Canada and sailed south on Lake Champlain. They took Fort Ticonderoga in July, and continued attacking into New York. **Colonial militiamen** surprised Burgoyne's force at the Battle of Bennington, in what is now Vermont, on August 16, 1777. The militiamen were dressed like civilians, and Burgoyne's forces wrongly assumed they were Loyalists. The Americans won the day, killing 200 and taking 700 prisoners. Burgoyne's force was weakened by the loss and was now running short of supplies.

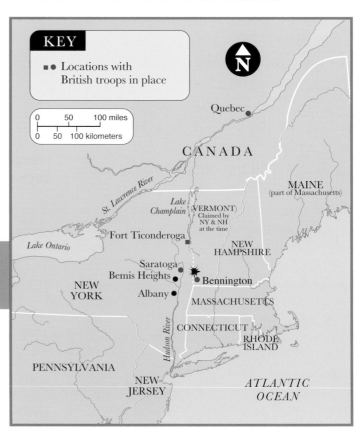

The British three-pronged attack of 1777 never happened as planned.

The Battle of Bennington on August 16, 1777 was an important victory for the Americans. General Burgoyne's forces suffered huge losses in both soldiers and supplies.

WHAT WENT WRONG?

The original British plan for the summer of 1777 was to make a three-pronged attack. The idea was to attack in New York and cut off the **New England** colonies from the others. The British thought that would end the war. The plan was for General Burgoyne to lead an army south from Canada to Albany, New York. General Howe would bring troops from New York City to meet them. British Colonel Barry St. Leger would approach Albany from the west.

The British Plan Fails

General Howe never received his orders for the plan. Instead, he set out to attack Washington and Philadelphia. Colonel St. Leger's forces laid **siege** to Fort Stanwix on their way to Albany. Benedict Arnold had spread rumors that he was leading a very large force. When St. Leger learned that Arnold was approaching, he became nervous and retreated. The British plan for a three-pronged attack failed.

British General Henry Clinton eventually left from New York City to bring troops to help Burgoyne. After capturing forts along the way, Clinton began to worry about New York City. He decided to turn back to protect his headquarters there.

General Burgoyne crossed the Hudson River near Saratoga, New York, and continued toward Albany. General Horatio Gates positioned his **colonial** troops on Bemis Heights and blocked the road.

Battle of Bemis Heights

Burgoyne was running out of supplies and decided not to wait any longer for help. He took part of his army and attacked Bemis Heights. More **militiamen** had joined General Gates, and they were ready for Burgoyne's attack. They destroyed the British force, and the rest of Burgoyne's army withdrew.

British Surrender at Saratoga

The colonial troops chased the British up the Hudson River to Saratoga. Gates positioned his men to surround the British and block any chance of escape. On October 17, 1777, Burgoyne surrendered his entire army. As news of the victory spread, there was hope for the cause of independence.

The surrender at Saratoga was an embarrassment for the British. Burgoyne never commanded British troops after this.

General Howe's Letter

In Philadelphia, General Howe learned of Burgoyne's defeat. He spoke of its effect in a letter to Lord George Germain, British Secretary of State for the Colonies:

> "My Lord, in consequence of the misfortune that has fallen upon the troops under Lieutenant-General Burgoyne's command, a considerable **reinforcement** from General Gates's corps has joined General Washington. The hopes of the people at large as well as of the rebel army are greatly raised from this event…"

As British commander in chief, General Howe was blamed for the defeat at Saratoga. He returned to England to defend himself. General Sir Henry Clinton assumed command of the British Army in May 1778.

Turning Point

Great Britain was a long-time enemy of France. However, King Louis XVI (16th) did not want to support a lost cause. Then news came of the colonial victory at Saratoga. Benjamin Franklin was finally allowed to meet with the king. France became an important **ally** of the colonies. The French sent troops, money, and naval support to help the colonies fight the British.

KEY

- - - - - - Continental Army position

→ Continental Army route (chasing British to Saratoga)

→ British Army route

NEW YORK

Saratoga

Freeman's Farm

Bemis Heights

Mohawk River

City of Albany

Hudson River

N

0   10   20   30 miles

0   10 20 30 kilometers

The Continental Army chased British troops from Bemis Heights to Saratoga.

What Happened During the Winter at Valley Forge?

In December 1777, Washington led his men on a difficult march to Valley Forge, about 29 kilometers (18 miles) northwest of Philadelphia. The men began building rough huts out of mud and logs. This is where the Continental Army spent the winter. Conditions were horrible. Washington wrote to Congress, begging for the supplies his men badly needed.

Help for the Troops?

In February 1778, a volunteer from the German kingdom of Prussia named Friedrich Wilhelm Augustus, Baron von Steuben, arrived to help Washington. Von Steuben began a training program to make the troops a more disciplined fighting force. The Continental Army suffered through the winter and came out much stronger. Supplies finally arrived in the spring. More good news came in May, when word of the French promise of aid reached Valley Forge.

George Washington is pictured here on horseback on a snowy day at Valley Forge. Washington's troops trained there through the winter.

Battle of Monmouth

By June 1778, British General Henry Clinton decided to move his headquarters to New York City. Washington pursued the British. On June 28, 1778, they fought a battle near Monmouth Court House in New Jersey. Neither side could claim victory. However, this time it was the British Army that slipped away in the night. Washington's army proved it could now face the British troops in open battle. Clinton continued his retreat and arrived in New York in July.

WHAT WENT WRONG?

Joseph Plumb Martin was a young **colonial** soldier during the war. He wrote of the march to Valley Forge and condition of the men:

"The army was now not only starved but naked. The greatest part were shirtless and barefoot. They lacked blankets. I found a piece of raw cowhide and made myself a pair of moccasins. It was this or go barefoot, as hundreds of my companions had to, till they might be tracked by their blood upon the rough frozen ground."

Washington's army faced the British soldiers in open battle at Monmouth. The British then retreated.

Who Was John Paul Jones?

John Paul Jones commanded a small fleet of ships sent to attack British ports and **merchant** ships. On September 23, 1779, Jones was off the eastern coast of England, near Flamborough Head. He spotted a **convoy** of British merchant ships led by the *Serapis*, which was commanded by Captain Richard Pearson. The *Bonhomme Richard* was an older ship with 42 cannons. It was outmatched against the new, 44-cannon British **frigate** *Serapis*.

Jones had two other ships with him, the *Alliance* and the *Pallas*. Pearson had one other ship, the *Countess of Scarborough*. The *Pallas* and *Alliance* moved to attack the *Countess of Scarborough*. The *Bonhomme Richard* and *Serapis* moved to attack each other. Once in range, they both used their **broadside** cannons. The *Bonhomme Richard* was badly damaged.

The Battle Continues

Helped by a sudden wind, John Paul Jones positioned his damaged ship alongside the *Serapis*. His men tied the ships together. **Sharpshooters** on the *Bonhomme Richard* fired at the gun crews on the British ship. The *Serapis* continued to fire its cannons. The *Bonhomme Richard* caught fire. As night fell, the battle continued under a full moon. The *Alliance* fired on the *Bonhomme Richard* by mistake, causing even more damage.

Jones's own officers thought he should surrender to the *Serapis*, but Jones refused to give in.

Captain Pearson called for Jones to surrender, but Jones refused. The battle continued for more than three hours. The *Serapis* was damaged further. The *Alliance* moved into position and appeared ready to hit the *Serapis* with its cannons. Captain Pearson finally surrendered. Jones and the crew of the sinking *Bonhomme Richard* boarded the *Serapis*. The *Countess of Scarborough* surrendered moments later.

Primary Source:
Battle of Flamborough Head

This is a hand-colored etching of the Battle of Flamborough Head. It was the only naval battle of the Revolutionary War in which the captain who won the battle lost his ship.

Thinking About the Source:

What is the physical setting of this image?

If someone made this today, what would be different?

Where Did Fighting Take Place in the South?

In 1778, the British decided they needed to control the southern **colonies** of Georgia, South Carolina, and North Carolina. They could then use those colonies as bases from which to regain control of the ten remaining colonies. This plan relied on the strength of the British Navy. The British also thought they'd get help from southern **Loyalists**.

Battle of Savannah

In November 1778, Lieutenant Colonel Archibald Campbell sailed from New York City with 3,500 British soldiers. In December, near Savannah, Georgia, he defeated a force of that included about 150 **militiamen** led by colonial General Robert Howe. The British continued on to capture Augusta, gaining control of Georgia.

Polish General Casimir Pulaski was mortally wounded while fighting the British in the final part of the Battle of Savannah on October 9, 1779.

Battle of Charleston

The British then turned their attention to South Carolina. The Continental Army was positioned in Charleston, an important military base and port. British ships took positions along the coast.

The British Army surrounded Charleston. The British **siege** of Charleston lasted about a month. The outnumbered colonial troops surrendered control of the city on May 12, 1780.

Battle of Camden

After Charleston, the British plan to establish control in South Carolina was blocked by repeated attacks by local militia. General Horatio Gates was the newly appointed commander of the Southern Continental Army. He decided to attack the British **outpost** at Camden. However, the British surprised colonial forces by attacking first. They killed or captured nearly half of Gates's 4,000 troops.

This is a view of the siege of Charleston from British lines. When Charleston surrendered to the British, the colonists gave up about 4,000 troops and large amounts of weapons.

Even after victories at Charleston and Camden, the British could not control the South Carolina countryside. Lord Charles Cornwallis decided to invade North Carolina. He broke his British army into two parts. One part, commanded by Patrick Ferguson, traveled west to find Loyalist support. Cornwallis led the other part on a different route. The two groups planned to meet near Charlotte.

Battle of King's Mountain

Near the border between North and South Carolina, Ferguson's group of British **Loyalists** camped on King's Mountain. On October 7, 1780, a group of North Carolina **Patriots** went up the mountain and surrounded Ferguson. In the fighting that followed, the Patriots killed Ferguson and killed or captured most of his British force.

Battle of Cowpens

After the British defeat at King's Mountain, Cornwallis gave up his plan to invade North Carolina. He withdrew to Winnsboro, South Carolina, for the winter to wait for **reinforcements**. Nathanael Greene became the new commander of Continental forces in the South. Greene split his army into two groups. Daniel Morgan headed one, and the other was under Greene's command.

Cornwallis sent British troops, led by Banastre Tarleton, to stop Morgan. The two groups met in battle at Cowpens on January 17, 1781. Morgan placed two lines of **militiamen** in front of trained Continental soldiers. When the British attacked, the militia fired two **volleys** and retreated. The volleys slowed the British charge. The Continental soldiers then attacked the broken British line and defeated Tarleton's troops.

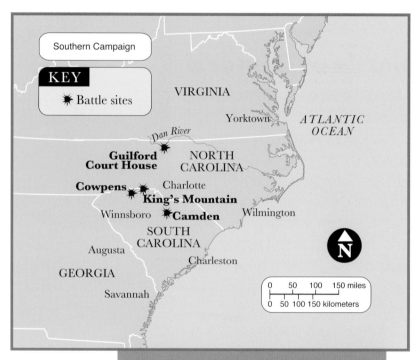

The British planned to capture the major southern cities and then move north. However, they were unable to gain control of the southern countryside.

Battle of Guilford Court House

The **colonial** groups under Greene and Morgan met and retreated northward. Cornwallis chased them until they crossed the Dan River into Virginia. The British then returned to North Carolina. Nathanael Greene carefully followed the British. The colonists received reinforcements near the town of Guilford Court House. The Patriots had about twice as many troops as the British when the British attacked.

At the end of the day, Cornwallis controlled the battlefield, but his army suffered great losses. Cornwallis headed to the coast to regroup. He then decided to attack Virginia and began marching there to meet reinforcements.

The Battle of Guilford Court House (pictured right) took place on March 15, 1781.

How Did the Americans Win at the Battle of Yorktown?

Cornwallis selected Yorktown, Virginia, as his base of operations. He arrived there in August 1781. By then, the French Army under the command of Jean-Baptiste Donatien de Vimeur, comte de Rochambeau, had joined forces with Washington in New York. They decided they did not have enough troops to lay **siege** to New York City. In mid-August, Rochambeau and Washington received a letter from French Admiral François Joseph Paul, comte de Grasse. De Grasse and the French Navy now had the authority to help them.

The New Plan

Rochambeau suggested that the French fleet of ships come and prevent Cornwallis from escaping Yorktown by sea. If Rochambeau and Washington could march their armies from New York to Virginia, they would be able to trap the British in Yorktown. Washington agreed to the plan. De Grasse's fleet set sail from the West Indies (islands in the Caribbean Sea), heading for the Chesapeake Bay.

French ships helped the Americans challenge British sea power.

Washington sent orders to Gilbert du Motier, Marquis de Lafayette, to keep Cornwallis in Yorktown. He also ordered half of the Continental Army to keep General Clinton and the British distracted in New York, so that they would not be able to send help to Cornwallis.

The French fleet arrived safely in the Chesapeake Bay. On September 5, Admiral de Grasse fought an outnumbered and outgunned British fleet. After about two hours, the badly damaged British fleet withdrew and sailed back to New York. The French fleet now had control of Chesapeake Bay. Cornwallis could no longer expect help by sea.

KEYS TO VICTORY

French assistance was a key to victory for the **Patriots** at Yorktown. The French Army under the command of Rochambeau strengthened Washington's Continental force. The small Continental fleet could not stand up to the British Navy. The French Navy was crucial for preventing a British escape by sea at Yorktown.

Primary Source: Marquis de Lafayette

The famous French volunteer, the Marquis de Lafayette, pinned down Cornwallis at Yorktown until the full Continental Army arrived.

Thinking About the Source:

What do you notice first about this image?

Do you think it's very different from other classic portraits done during the time? If so, which style of portrait do you prefer?

41

Siege of Yorktown

Washington, Rochambeau, and Lafayette combined their American and French forces for a total of about 16,000 troops. Cornwallis had fewer than 8,000 British troops, and the French Navy blocked his chance for **reinforcements**. During the first weeks of October, the Continental and French Armies bombarded British troops in Yorktown day and night.

On October 16, Cornwallis attempted to escape across the York River. A violent storm prevented the British from crossing and forced them to return to Yorktown. The next day, with over 100 heavy guns pointed at him, Cornwallis had to give up. On October 19, 1781, the British troops marched out of Yorktown and laid down their weapons in surrender.

Battle of Eutaw Springs

Before this, on September 8, 1781, Nathanael Greene attacked a British force at Eutaw Springs in South Carolina. There was heavy fighting, and Greene's army was forced to withdraw. However, British losses were severe, and they retreated to Charleston. The Battle of Eutaw Springs helped break the British hold in the South. It also ensured that the British could not send help to Cornwallis at Yorktown.

Victory!

News of the British surrender reached Philadelphia on October 22. The city joyfully celebrated. The same news reached London in late November. The British had large debts from the war. They were also fighting the French and Spanish in the West Indies. They did not have more soldiers available. The British realized they had to give up the thirteen American **colonies**.

Minor battles continued for eighteen months before peace talks began. After eight years of war, peace negotiations took place in Paris, France. An agreement was signed on September 3, 1783, officially ending the Revolutionary War. Colonial independence from Great Britain was finally recognized. The United States now faced the challenge of surviving and growing as an independent nation.

After the British left, George Washington and his troops returned to New York City in victory. Spectators lined the streets to welcome them.

Timeline

1763	Treaty of Paris signed (ending French and Indian War)
1764	Sugar Act passed
1765	Stamp Act passed
1765	Quartering Act passed
	Sons of Liberty formed
1766	Stamp Act repealed
	Parliament passes Declaratory Acts
1767	Townshend Acts passed
1770	Boston Massacre (March 5)
1773	Tea Act passed
	Boston Tea Party (December 16)
1774	Intolerable Acts passed
	First Continental Congress meets
1775	Paul Revere and William Dawes warn colonists that the British are coming
	Battles of Lexington and Concord (April 19)
	Second Continental Congress meets
	George Washington appointed commander of Continental Army
	Battle of Bunker Hill (June 17)
	Defeat at Quebec (December 30)
1776	Thomas Paine writes *Common Sense*
	Siege of Boston ends
	Declaration of Independence signed (July 4)
	New York falls to the British
	Battle of Trenton, New Jersey (December 26)
1777	Battle of Princeton, New Jersey (January 3)
	Fort Ticonderoga falls to the British (July 5)
	Battle of Bennington (August 16)
	Battle of Brandywine (September 11)
	Philadelphia falls to the British (September 26)
	Battle of Germantown (October 4)

	Battle of Saratoga (October 7)
	British General Burgoyne surrenders (October 17)
	Congress passes Articles of Confederation (November 15)
	Winter of Washington's army at Valley Forge
1778	France declares war and joins the Patriot cause
	Battle of Monmouth Courthouse (June 28)
	Savannah captured by the British (December 29)
1779	George Rogers Clark captures Vincennes (February 25) in the Western frontier
	Naval battle of John Paul Jones's *Bonhomme Richard* against the British warship *Serapis* (September 23)
1780	Charleston, South Carolina, falls to the British (May 12)
	Battle of Camden (August 16)
	Battle of Kings Mountain (October 7)
1781	Battle of Cowpens (January 17)
	Articles of Confederation adopted by the states (March 1)
	Battle of Guilford Courthouse (March 15)
	Battle of Eutaw Springs (September 8)
	Cornwallis and the British surrender at Yorktown, Virginia (October 19)
1783	Treaty of Paris signed, ending the war (September 3)
	Continental Army disbanded, and Washington retires from the military
1785	Congress establishes dollar as official currency
1786	Shay's Rebellion
1787	Northwest Ordinance
	Constitutional Convention meets
	Constitution signed (September 17)
1788	Federalist Papers
	Constitution is ratified
1789	First meeting of Congress
	George Washington sworn in as first president
1791	Congress adopts the Bill of Rights as the first ten amendments to the Constitution

Glossary

ally country that agrees to help another country in a war

artillery large guns such as cannons; the part of the army that uses the large guns

bayonet long knife that is attached to the end of a rifle

boycott refuse to buy something or do something as a way of protesting

broadside attack in which all the guns on one side of a ship are fired at the same time

colony area that is under the political control of a more powerful country that is usually far away

commodore high rank in the navy, in charge of a group of ships

Continental Congress group of men who represented the thirteen colonies during the time of the Revolutionary War; its members are often called the "Founding Fathers"

convoy group of ships or vehicles traveling together, sometimes for protection

enlistment time in the military; to enlist is to join the military

French and Indian War name for fighting that took place 1754–1763 in North America between the French and the British

frigate small, fast ship used in wars to protect other ships

garrison group of soldiers living in a town or fort and defending it

guerilla style of fighting where small groups attack and then escape, rather than facing the enemy in open battle

Hessian soldier from German state of Hesse-Cassel who served in the British Army in the Revolutionary War

Intolerable Acts name colonists gave to the Coercive Acts of 1774, which included several acts

Loyalist person who remained loyal to Great Britain during the Revolutionary War

merchant someone who buys and sells goods in large amounts; merchant ships transport goods

militia group of people who act as soldiers but are not part of the professional army; also called militiamen

New England area of the northeastern United States that includes Maine, New Hampshire, Vermont, Massachusetts, Rhode Island, and Connecticut

outpost group of buildings not in a town or city that are established as a military camp or place of trade

Parliament main lawmaking group in Great Britain

Patriot person who supported independence from Great Britain during the Revolutionary War

rebellion organized attempt to change the government or leadership of a country by using violence

reinforcements more soldiers sent to a battle or war to make their group stronger

sharpshooter someone very skilled at aimed shooting with a gun

siege situation in which an army surrounds a place to try to gain control of it or force someone out of it

Sons of Liberty secret groups formed in the colonies before the Revolutionary War that included people who protested British taxes and supported independence from Great Britain

Stamp Act act in 1765 that required a tax to be paid when paper documents were made or sold; each item had to be stamped as proof that the tax had been paid

Sugar Act act in 1764 that taxed molasses shipped to colonial ports and prevented colonies from importing molasses from other countries

Tea Act act in 1773 that made the East India Company the only company allowed to sell tea in the American colonies, with Parliament collecting a tax on it

territory land that is controlled by a particular country or ruler

Townshend Acts acts in 1767 that placed taxes on items brought into the colonies, including glass, lead, paper, and tea

traitor person who betrays or is disloyal to a person or country

volley large number of bullets shot through the air at the same time

Find Out More

Books

Anderson, Dale. *Key Battles of the American Revolution, 1776–1778*. Milwaukee, WI: Gareth Stevens, 2005.

Murray, Stuart. *American Revolution*. New York: DK Children, 2005.

Tarbox Raatma, Lucia. *African American Soldiers in the Revolutionary War*. Mankato, MN: Compass Point Books, 2009.

Websites

http://www.historyforkids.org/learn/northamerica/after1500/history/revolution.htm
This site, run by Kidipede, provides all kinds of links discussing different ideas and events of the Revolutionary War.

http://www.pbs.org/ktca/liberty/
This PBS site discusses the American Revolution and matches a TV series aired by PBS called "Liberty! The American Revolution," which is also available on DVD.

http://kids.yahoo.com/directory/Around-the-World/Countries/United-States/History/Colonial-Life-(1585-1783)/American-Revolutionary-War
This Yahoo! Kids site has useful links to other sites that discuss the Revolutionary War.

DVDs

Liberty! The American Revolution (DVD). Hosted by news anchor Forrest Sawyer and narrated by Edward Herrmann. PBS DVD Video, 1997.

The Revolution (DVD). History Channel DVDs, 2006.

Index